KT-418-922

CONTENTS

Skateboarding is.................4

Then........................6

And now.....................8

Decks 10

Street style 12

Park life.....................14

Ramp it up 16

Demos and comps 18

From the ground up 20

Flips.........................22

Grind on......................24

Your domain 26

Road to sponsorship...........28

Need to know words 30

Skateboard heroes/
Skateboarding online 31

Index.........................32

WARNING!

The tricks featured in this book have
been performed by experienced skateboarders.
Neither the publisher nor the author shall be liable for
any bodily harm or damage to property that may
happen as a result of trying the tricks in this book.

In many places it is illegal to skateboard.
Look out for signs. Don't break the law.

NO SKATEBOARDING

SKATEBOARDING IS...

...a secret world!

Skateboarding has its own language.
It has its own heroes. It also has its own music
and its own art – graffiti.

Skateboarding will change the way that
you look at the streets.

Welcome to the underground world of
skateboarding.

"I love skateboarding. It helps me be me. It's how I feel free."

Skateboarder Rodney Mullen: he invented the kickflip by accident – he was trying an ollie.

Skateboarding was invented in the late 1960s in the USA.

Bored surfers began skateboarding when there were no waves out at sea.
They carved up the streets of California.
Soon an army of skateboarders grew!

Skateboarding was even in the 1970s TV show

The ollie is the most important trick to learn.
It was invented by Alan 'Ollie' Gelfand in 1977.
You need to ollie to be able to do most tricks.

The ollie helps you to get the board off the ground.

OLLIE

Kick down on the tail of the board.
At the same time, drag your front
foot up the griptape. As you do this,
you must jump as well.

...AND NOW

Now, people skateboard all over the world.

Many skateboarders are professional. This means they earn money doing it!

Skateboarding appears in video games and music videos. Skateboarders listen to a lot of music. They love hip-hop and heavy metal.

"I felt like I'd made it when I appeared in a video game."
Paul Rodriguez, street skater

Skateboarding and art go hand in hand. Many skaters go to art college. Some are very good graffiti artists.

Anything goes in skateboarding fashion.
Skaters wear baggy jeans, tight jeans,
sweatpants or shorts. There are thousands
of shoe designs to choose from, too.

DECKS

The graphics on skateboard decks are changing all the time. Professional riders choose their own unique design.

The graphics on your deck can tell other riders something about your style and who you are.

Griptape is a sandpaper type material. It helps the rider's feet grip the deck.

Trucks attach the wheels to the deck. They help you make turns.

Wheel

STREET STYLE

Many people start ripping up the streets when they first discover skateboarding. They use street furniture to do tricks.

SKATESPEAK

Street furniture – Curbs, park benches, stairs and handrails.

Street decks are
thin and small,
with small,
light wheels.

PARK LIFE

Many towns have skateparks with halfpipes, bowls and other obstacles.

Skateboarders use the obstacles to perform flips, spins and grabs high in the air.

HALFPIPE

Skateparks are ideal places to hook up with friends. You can show off your new tricks. You can also see local heroes killing the obstacles.

BOWL

Dinosaur parks – Old, concrete skateparks that were built in the 1970s.
Mini-ramp – A small half-pipe about 1.5 metres high.

RAMP IT UP

A vert ramp is a big halfpipe about 3.5 metres high. Helmets and pads are a must for this type of skateboarding.

VERT RAMP

Vert ramps are where skateboarders learn to fly!

Helmet

Elbow pads

Shorts allow the skater to wear knee pads.

Vert decks are wider than street decks. This gives better control and stability.

Big wheels gain more speed. They also help when touching back down to earth.

DEMOS AND COMPS

Skateboard competitions are held all over the world.

You will get to see skateboard superstars and top skateboard team demos.

At the end of a demo, the teams throw out free stickers, t-shirts and even decks!

So make sure you stay until the end!

The vert section of a vert ramp is vertical – it goes straight up!

FROM THE GROUND UP

Beginner skateboarders are called grommets.

To become a great skateboarder you will need to learn some basic tricks, such as ollies, flips and grinds.

KICKFLIP

A kickflip is where the board spins 360 degrees around its length underneath you. After it has spun, you need to land back on the board.

GRIND

To perform a grind, you must rub your trucks across the rail. When both trucks are grinding, you are doing a 50–50 grind.

SKATESPEAK

Fakie – Travelling backwards.
Gnarly – Dangerous or extreme.
Goofy – Standing right foot forward.
Rad – Super good.
Regular – Standing left foot forward.
Ripping – Skateboarding very well.
Sick – Good.
Slam – When you fall off your board.

FLIPS

There are many types of flips. They will have you kicking and spinning into old age. Here are some difficult ones.

360 FLIP

The board spins 360 degrees and flips at the same time.

BACKSIDE FLIP

The board flips and turns 180 degrees. You follow the board and ride away backwards.

FAKIE KICKFLIP

This is a kickflip going backwards.

Rad!

The trucks of your deck can be used to grind along edges and rails.

It's a tricky combo of power and balance.

NOSE GRIND

A nose grind is when you rub just the front truck on a rail.

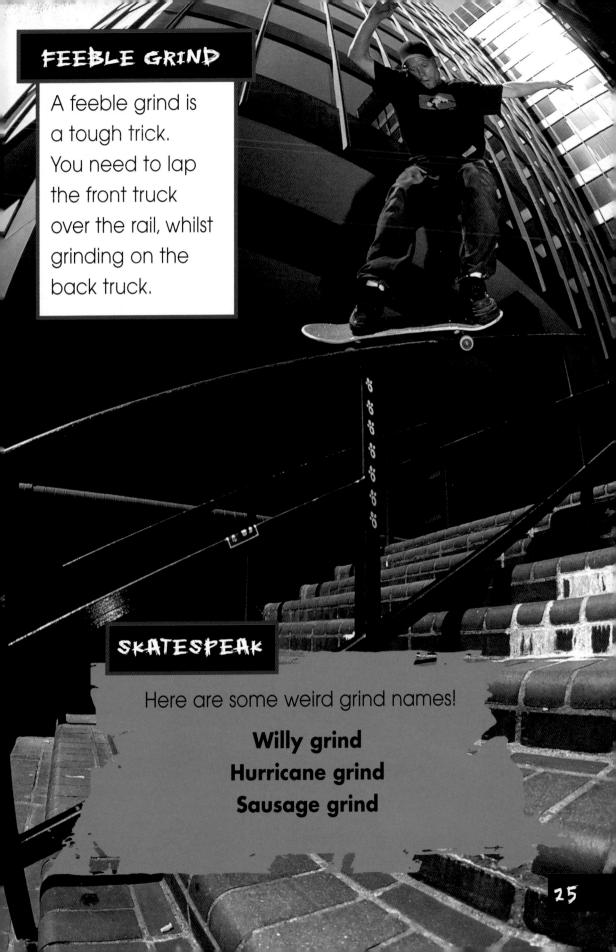

FEEBLE GRIND

A feeble grind is a tough trick. You need to lap the front truck over the rail, whilst grinding on the back truck.

SKATESPEAK

Here are some weird grind names!

Willy grind
Hurricane grind
Sausage grind

YOUR DOMAIN

The streets and skateparks where you live are now your domain.

Time to explore!

WALLRIDE TO FAKIE

Ramps will allow you to fly like a bird.

KICKFLIP

Stairs are no longer just to walk up and down

Maybe kickflip them!

50-50 GRINDS

Handrails become train tracks for 50–50 grinds.

If you learn some good tricks you can film them. Then you can make a 'sponsor me' tape.

Send the tape to your favourite skateboard company. If they like your moves, they'll send you free stuff, such as brand new skateboards and t-shirts.

Professional skateboarders get paid to skate! Their sponsorship company will send them all over the world to enter competitions. They also get a board with their own unique graphics.

Top pro Tony Hawk has his own movie company, computer game and a range of clothing.

NEED TO KNOW WORDS

carve To turn sharply on your board.

demo A skateboard team showing off their moves.

domain Your area. The places you skate most often.

graffiti Colourful drawings and words created with spray paint cans.

graphics The pictures or designs on the underside of the deck.

hook up Skatespeak for meeting up with friends.

killing it Skatespeak for skating at a very high standard.

obstacles Halfpipes, ramps, stairs – anything that you can skateboard on.

ollie A skateboard jump. The ollie is the best way to get all four wheels off the ground. Hit the tail and jump in the air.

professional The best of the best! Skateboarders who get paid to skate by a skateboard company.

skateparks Indoor or outdoor parks designed for skateboarding. Obstacles in the park can be made from concrete, wood and sometimes even metal.

sponsorship When a company gives a skateboarder free stuff, such as decks. If you are really good, a company may pay you to skate for them and advertise their products.

stability Making something stable so it isn't wobbly.

trucks The metal parts that fix the wheels to the deck.

underground To be alternative and outside the mainstream.

unique The only one of its kind.

SKATEBOARD HEROES

Tony Hawk has set up a foundation to help pay for skateboard parks in low-income areas in the USA. The *Tony Hawk Foundation* has raised over £850,000 for skateparks.

In 2004, Danny Way broke his own world record for the longest skateboard jump. It's now set at 24 metres! In 2005, Danny jumped across the Great Wall of China on a skateboard.

Check out:
http://www.dannyway.com/_videos/dw_china_Med.mov

SKATEBOARDING ONLINE

Websites

http://www.mpora.com

http://www.how2skate.com/

http://www.sidewalkmag.com/

http://www.blueprintskateboards.com/

INDEX

B
bowls 14

C
California 6
clothes 9, 17, 29
competitions 18-19, 29

D
decks 10-11, 13, 17, 19, 30
demos 18-19, 30

F
flips 14, 20, 22-23

G
Gelfand, Alan 'Ollie' 7
graffiti 4, 8, 30
graphics 10-11, 29
grinds 20, 21, 24-25, 27
griptape 11
grommets 20

H
halfpipes 14, 16-17,
Hawk, Tony 29, 31
heavy metal music 8
helmets 16-17
hip-hop music 8

I
invention of skateboarding 6

K
kickflips 5, 20, 27

M
mini-ramps 15
music 4, 8

O
ollies 5, 7, 20, 30

P
pads 13, 16-17
professional skateboarders
    8, 11, 29, 30

S
skate parks 14-15, 30
skatespeak 4, 12, 21, 25, 26
sponsorship 28-29, 30
street furniture 12, 24-25
street style 12-13, 26-27
streets 4, 6, 26

T
tricks 7, 20-21, 22-23, 24-25,
    26-27
trucks 11, 24-25, 30

U
underground world 4, 30

V
vert ramps 16-17, 18-19
video games 8, 29

W
Way, Danny 31
wheels 11, 13, 17